Elegy for ETHERIDGE

Elegy for ETHERIDGE

POEMS

PINKIE GORDON LANE

Louisiana State University Press   *Baton Rouge*

MM

For my son, GORDON

Copyright © 1970, 1972, 1977, 1978, 1981, 1985, 1991,
1993, 1997, 2000 by Pinkie Gordon Lane
All rights reserved
Manufactured in the United States of America

First printing
09 08 07 06 05 04 03 02 01 00
5 4 3 2 1

Designer: Barbara Neely Bourgoyne
Typeface: Adobe Garamond
Printer and binder: Thomson-Shore, Incorporated

Library of Congress Cataloging-in-Publication Data

Lane, Pinkie Gordon.
    Elegy for Etheridge : poems / Pinkie Gordon Lane.
    p. cm.
    ISBN 0-8071-2544-X (alk. paper) — ISBN 0-8071-2545-8 (pbk. : alk. paper)
    I. Title

PS3562.A4845 E+

                                                99-058655
                                                CIP

The author offers grateful acknowledgment to the editors of the following publications,
in which some of the poems in this book originally appeared: *African American Review,*
*Black Scholar, Louisiana English Journal, Louisiana Review, Ms. Magazine, South and
West: An International Literary Quarterly,* and *Xavier Review.* Poems also appeared in
Louisiana Laurels, ed. Donald Stanford (Arts Council of Greater Baton Rouge, 1991);
and in the author's *I Never Scream* (Lotus Press, 1985), *The Mystic Female* (South and
West, 1978), and *Wind Thoughts* (South and West, 1972).

The paper in this book meets the guidelines for permanence and durability of the
Committee on Production Guidelines for Book Longevity of the Council on Library
Resources. ∞

Contents

III

I

VIOLINS

For Dinos Constantinides

I love violins.
If violins were people,
they would dance like Debbie,
sing like Mattiwilda,
poet like Rita.*

They would leave one long
line of remembrance—
a balancing act of recall—
or one departing wish
to pass on to
        the compassionately loved,
        the tenderly touched.

Those delicately piercing strings
would reach into every corner
of a world still raw to the bone
and make a magic of healing
with music that calls up colors of violet
or blue, becomes a canvas of the space
in between.

Violins transform darkness
into light, yet know
that chiaroscuro lends character
and form, that pianissimo
and fortissimo capture the moment,
sending forth sounds touching
nerves of response,
        sending us soaring
        like doves, like eagles
           into a sky's winter night—

---

*Debbie Allen, Mattiwilda Dobbs, and Rita Dove.

like the poem
whose words remain dormant
till taught to sing
by the violin's flight.

On Being Head of the English Department

I will look with detachment
on the signing of contracts,
the ordering of books,
and making of schedules—
will sing hymns of praise
to the negative, when
it is necessary to survive.

And if the morning
light freezes in the east,
a dawn-covered sky
will tell me I am cold
to your pleas, but never whore
to the spirit. I will
write poems in the blue
frosted lake.

If I disdain poetasters,
announcers, and the gods
of mediocrity, knowing
that they, too, insist on living,
it is because I hand you
the bread and the knife
but never the music and art
of my existence.

You will not swallow me or absorb me:
I have grown too lean for that.
I am selfish, I am cruel,

I am love.

When You Read This Poem

*For Citizens Opposed to Book
Censorship, Baton Rouge, La.*

The earth turns
like a rainbow
And the smell of autumn
drifts down   Yellow
leaf on my arched back

The light touches
I see it with my skin
feel it lean
That furrow of trees
casts its shadow—long
as the night, the wind,
the river

Truth has many faces
My friends, don't honor me
without passion
I will not be wheat in the summer's fire
I will not lie fallen
like autumn fruit
or die in the evening sun

Listen,
let us band together
and fight evil   We
cannot let it burn
the earth   We
cannot let it guide
the sun

The world is a bird
in flight

When you read this poem,
love me

MESSAGE

To the brother who thinks that poets should stop writing.
National Conference of African-American Writers,
Howard University, Washington, D.C.

I have found my voice
in the attic
in the silence of closed rooms
in the night winds raging
I am a stranger,
a thief, who follows sound
with ears

Mama's knees no longer hurt
for they have grown an outer skin
and her woolly hair
is pinned back at the neck
One by one she watched her loves
turn to dust: music,
color, poetry

I listen to rain—
its deep tones
are like night air after supper
when voices run faster
than thoughts
or children playing in the streets

Lovers, gather your bones
Don't let them vanish
in spaces
Listen

Listen
we cannot be without grace
like those who have forgotten
love

My friends, listen,
I cannot take from you
more than I give
Did you think I would
diminish you?

       Hear
the beating of hearts
in the harvest of music
whose song is a message
is life
Listen

       Listen

Sexual Privacy of Women on Welfare

The ACLU Mountain States Regional Office came across a welfare application used in [a certain state] for women with illegitimate children. Among the questions:
—When and where did you first meet the defendant [the child's father].
—When and where did intercourse first occur.
—Frequency and period of time during which intercourse occurred.
—Was anyone else ever present. If yes, give dates, names, and addresses.
—Were preventive measures always used.
—Have you had intercourse with anyone other than the defendant.
—If yes, give the dates, names, and addresses.

> —*The Privacy Report,* American Civil Liberties Union Foundation,
> vol. 4, no. 3, Oct. 1976

When and where did you first
confront loneliness?
When and where did you resist
the urge to die?
Did you pull a blind around
your sorrow?
Was anyone present? If yes, give
names and dates and addresses.
Did you survive?
Were preventive measures always
used?
Who listened to the rage of your
silent screams? Give the frequency
and period of time,
dates and names and addresses . . .

Will you promise never to breathe ice?
To follow the outline
of a city street whose perspective
darkens with the morning light?

Document.

LYRIC

When the wind shifts,
I'll marry you.
Out of the corner of my eye,
I'll marry you.

The wind and rain and yellow
leaves beat madness
into the midnight trail.

When the wind wraps a rope
around the sun, I'll
marry you—beneath
orchids and bending trees
and ice like thunder.

This is where the river ends.
This is where the sky turns red
and drops into the ocean's
depth. When the wind
stops in midair and shifts
to water's edge,

I'll marry you.

I HAVE FORGOTTEN

I have forgotten how to write
a love poem, forgotten
the feel of your touch,
your hands feathers
against my skin, tiny
prickles siphoning my nerves.

Forgotten your smile,
the wicked curve of your lips
as you string my hair—
your fingers snakes
in a tangled nest.

Forgotten your words of love,
your voice falling like leaves
on a wet autumn day.

Forgotten
your tears of remembrance—
eyes raining pools, your
trembling voice a mystery,
a song, a mountain stream
trickling, rushing, disappearing
into a wood void.

I have forgotten how to write
a love poem, forgotten
to forget to love you
no more—

to wash you from my
unbridled web of thought,
breast, loins.

Yes, I have forgotten how to write
a love poem, have
forgot, forgot,
forgot . . .

A CHRISTMAS TALE

Buy Christmas or sell it
or leave it dangling like a leaf
about to fall. At any rate
we are stuck with it. It
is our legacy, our albatross,
our gift for good givers,
our rain tree in a high wind.

I think of it as winter,
and change, and transition—
a dream for tomorrow.

All the Christmases of Christmas
past have ganged up on us.
They say: "Give your gifts
of gold to the poor,
to the old, the infirm.

"Hang rice on a tree.
But remember the BRIGHT STAR'S
FIRE—the beginning of legend,
cracked asunder, spirals
in the orbit of this revolving
time."

On This Louisiana Day

On this Louisiana day
I tell you to come up
from heaven.

Mahalia sings her way
to glory, and the raped
girls of Bangladesh weep

for their spread loins
and wish the babies in their wombs
were pearls.

Winter's autumn spans
the season and I . . .
I grasp four-cornered

twilight. Smiling faces
ask: Who loves me?
their eyes

round with wide despair
loving like a dove, and wishing
all the light would come.

POEM FOR SUE OWEN

Who sings of *Nursery
Rhymes for the Dead*
and *The Book of Winter.*

Pure is your voice,
throwing slant light
on walls.

You have found your place—your own
calligraphy of words.

Your name is "snow,"
owl, mouse, gray slate
of mountain, green of sea,
purple evening, and
scarlet night.

Your name is "snow."

ELEGY FOR ETHERIDGE

what now:
what now dumb nigger damn near dead
what now
now that you won't dance
behind the pale white doors of death. . . .
Your mama sitting in a quiet corner
praying to a white/jesus to save her black boy
     —From "Another Poem for Me (after Recovering
        from an O.D.)" by Etheridge Knight

who knew the knight
of prison, whose poems
from that unholy place made
Hard Rock immortal—

who sang the songs of ancestry,
who was linked to the clan, and yet
had "no sons to float
in the space between"—

who rode that trestle
till the end of his days,
whose songs were a spirit,
a "high," a *raison d'être* that
"literally saved my life," he said,
whose "soul [wanted] to sing"—

> Etheridge, like Pooky Dee who rode
> that trestle above his head
> daring death with each breath
> he took,

> *your* silence now "rolls like oil
> across the wide green water,"
> and you *now* "dance behind the pale
> white doors of death." Your mama

no longer need pray to a "white/
jesus to save her black boy."

You left us your songs
    to mourn your death
    to mourn your life,

to say the prayer that
    could not stop your headlong
    final plunge.

Etheridge, you dreamer and creator
of lines, you told us that
"Black Poets should live . . ."
are
    ". . . The Flutes of Black Lovers
    . . . The organs of Black Sorrows
    . . . The dust of marching feet."

Why did you leave us this space,
this emptiness, this BELLY SONG,
this prayer, this grave stone,
this chant of death for the dead?

Now, all we can say is:
    Etheridge, we loved you.
    Good-bye, good-bye, good-
    bye . . .

Letter to a Son: A Prose Poem

For Gordon

With an absolute *must* and a sense of rivalry, we reach out to the daughter or son—that untamed spirit thrusting upon itself the challenge of perfection, even when we know the impossibility of its attainment, that the striving for it is an albatross.

My son, you say that you have spent your entire life trying to live up to my expectations, never able to please me, always striving to accomplish that impossible feat—your soft, pointed chin projecting the image of yourself, like the rudder of a sailboat pushing stubbornly on even in the rush of a high wind.

And when the day comes that you reach the absolute perfection of imperfection, you will understand my cradling of your dreams in your own perverse skull, cherishing every nuance of your striving to be the perfect-imperfect creation, and loving you selflessly. You will come finally to realize that no action of yours, no scudding in what you thought was failure but which I knew was part of your "becoming," that no unedited thought of you was wasted.

Each atom, each molecule of you became something of the whole —beautiful in the molding, the rearranging, the reaching towards the actualization of what you are today, of what you will become tomorrow: and that this is an absolutely perfect-imperfect neverending story.

Another Poem for Gordon

Moving into his first purchased home

My son awakens with the chirping
of birds high in trees just outside his window.
Bedroom embraces all sounds.
Sun grazes his chin.

He has just purchased this old house—
well lived-in, waiting for the next
century to rattle its walls.

Gordon smiles, relaxed. This private
space lifts his spirits.

    Drummer, poet, artist—rise
    with the sun, this promise
    of a new day. Let your spirit
    soar. No time for sorrow,
    no time for grief, no time
    for recriminations. Sail
    with the resonance of your drums.
    Let cymbals ring forth a new day.
    Ride above clouds.

    Fly!   Fly!   Fly!

DYING

Poems for Ulysses Simpson Lane

I. SLUMBERING BATS

Death lies over this house
like an emaciated giant
uncertain as to where to rest
his hoary head.
I look cross-eyed at
blossoms drooping in the sun,
hanging like slumbering bats.

              Spring has a way
of stumbling in like an
inebriated old man. I cling
to living things—a kitten
in a furry ball at my feet,
shepherd dogs that rumble
like steam engines,
a pot of flowers clinging vinelike,
a wall's shadow racing
aimlessly with crooked fingers.

              Old men marry
young girls half their age
in self-denial of
the broken cage . . .
I surround myself with life
and watch bellies
fatten like earthworms,
bulge like happy pigs—
dumb brutes
positive in their blindness
that they will live forever.

II. FINIS # 1

The plane's motor roars
like a forest fire
Wings spread eagle, boxed
high over a sprawling scroll of land
It is his dying day
his millennium
hell's exit

I sit and listen to the sounds of talking
Someone is eating
Coughing scratches the dim silence beyond
The motor now becomes platitude
The sign on the wing says
"no step"
and the throb in my flesh
beats "no step," "no entrance"

It is the journey past thought

III. FINIS # 2

See how the jasmine
leans to the sky.
A blue-pink petal
selects a space of air
to hide the ominous
shadow of death.

I lean forward, smell
the sour/sweet odor
of summer rain caught
just beneath the frilled
edges of clustered blooms.

Beyond this space, this
effusion of color,
the pale glow of twilight
spreads beneath
the crimson
sky.

Found Poems

I. COMBAT ZONE

Time magazine, Feb. 20, 1984, p. 34

As darkness fell, the combat
grew in the savage street

Afraid of what the night
would bring, many sought
refuge   Every minute
seemed to bring the sound of
rockets   Even the usual
wail of crisis could not be
heard

Fire trucks did not risk
making runs

II. STRANGERS

The Morning Advocate, Baton Rouge, La.,
Feb. 20, 1984, pp. 1-A, 6-A

Monty and Julie died the night
of September 23, each with a bullet
in the head   They were found
on the seat of a new Datsun
parked near a city housing project

The car's ceiling light was
burning   A white poodle
was on Julie's lap

Shooting is a way to fill
an afternoon   The fear
of crimes of violence

is not just a fear of injury
or death

It is the fear of strangers

    I sleep with the light
    on now

III. GANGSTA RAP

    Time magazine, March 24, 1997, pp. 46–47

Life was sweet, good,
like something out of a
song   Then
he discovered gangsta rap

Records bearing his name
sold out in stores   Americans
have long been drawn
to the symbiosis between life
and pop culture

    This has gone too far, he says
    It's making us look like animals, he says
    I guess we hit the snooze button, he says
    It's just entertainment, he says

Violence, even the threat of it,
seems to feed on itself

Inside the hip-hop community
paranoia is running at high levels
Rumors are flying
The value of life is decreasing

    It's time to give people their dreams back,

he says

Body Language

My body, my life,
speaks, and I listen.

It is a tyrant that knows
my every mood. It tells me to laugh,
to cry, to dance, to
sing.

I revere you—soul of my soul.
I am laughing in pounds of water,
flesh, and bone—for
you know my secrets
of stretching taut like a serpent,
of bending in sinewy places,
of lying still like a stone.

You say:

> "Honor me,
> and I'll make you queen
> of your space. Abuse me
> and you'll raise
> the dead with your
> howlings and cries."

And you say:

> "I am the sister
> of spirit and light-rising,
> an angel guiding you
> into wholeness of SELF
> and reverence for health."

My body speaks, and I listen.

I genuflect to my body,
my tyrant, my teacher,
my guide, my loving
reflection. It is my
mirror, my canvas,

my clear stream on the mountainside,
my center of all that I am:

body and soul combined
in fire, in spirit, and in
life.

II

Two Owl Poems

I. OWL: A PAINTING

In an iron frame.
Rounded eyes sadly
staring, as if measuring
the air. A witch's beak.

A collar of downy white
outlines the head,
and extended undergrowth
camouflages feet that clutch,
balancing an oval form.

Why is this bird framed
in a cage, imprisoned—
the dark spirit howling,

unshackled, untamed, free?
No paint on canvas can
harness that power,

and flight is only
a dream away.

II. OWL

> And her wings straining suddenly aspread
> —Robert Frost

Suddenly, wings aspread,
she swoops, clutches
an early mouse
among leaves and limbs—
disappears in shadow and light.

I stand on wet ground,
smell the rain, taste the air—
only the memory of owl and mouse
remains.

GULLS

For Joanne

We saw them, Joanne,
spreading their slant wings
kite-fashion
and watched them glide
precision-aimed, and then
dip into the bay.

Wet-feathered, yet buoyant,
they burst from the ocean
skyward, then leveled off
only to dive again like
earthbound rockets.

We gazed in lulled fascination
only because we had nothing
else to do, because
we sought cessation of thought,
because we wanted to glide
from bay tide to peace
to extension of self
to sky and gulf and sea

to the ecstasy of tidedrift . . .

HALLET'S PEAK

Rocky Mountains, Colorado

What thousand-eyed wind
swept through your stone
hollowing out snow-filled gorge
and separating rock pinioned
against a gray crystal sky?

Blue spruce hug your base
and spread out like a skirt
tumbling into waters
of Bear Lake
sending back reflections
raised against the sun.

Your summit (a sharp
peak, sectioned in three
slate-slanted ridges
folding to a pyramidal angle)
knifes the cloudless sky
and your rounded base
bellies the hills
swelling distant firs.

My camera catches movement.
But my brush and palette
capture stillness, intimate
and buried in earth-moving
shadows shifting slowly
as rust-pink slips to lavender
before the day is done.

TRAIL RIDGE ROAD

America's highest continuous motor road,
Rocky Mountains National Park, Colorado

This coil spiraling itself
to an infernal blue heaven
looks over green angling contours
deceptively buoyant,
dangerously steep.

At twelve thousand feet I pause
and survey the peaks below
spreading out in massive spruce-
coated needles of green.

An ice-blue lake (pocket-sized below)
mirrors itself against the sky.
Chilling breezes are air-flung,
and brazen eagles sweep so close
I see black and white and red
feathers lift
in wind-swollen air.

I throw snowballs
in the middle of July.

My invasion of this altitude
of yellow tundra, chipmunks, mice,
and flying things whose names
I'll never know
borrows and returns
unsolicited.

CAMPANILE

For my young student poets,
University of Northern Iowa

Listen,
do you hear the wind?

Do you see the light
from the window
slanting inward, its beams
in beads, in threads
on shadow-tinted walls?

We are reminded of evergreens
in winter—snow-sculptured
forms marking the way
to towering structures
breaking space—
backdrops for trees
and shrubs.

The bell tower, lonely and lean,
tolls the nine o'clock hour.
And a cloudless sky
slants westward, pulled
by the evening sun.

It is a night owl on the wing
echoing my thoughts
while shadows
reign.

NIGHT SCENE

Firing into the night,
into the darkness, into the crash
of waves, the moon casts
its soundless voice—
a light beneath the sea.

I wander into this mirrored
scene, the wailing
and thrashing of foam,
the ocean-scented seaweed and flotsam
making their own design,
riding their own cadence and flow.

The white light of the moon,
the blue steam of the waves,
the beat of my heart rising
in stillness—reach for their center,
for their focal point, as a voice
in the distance blends
with the sigh and ebb of the
night.

EULOGY ON THE DEATH OF TREES

They are bulldozing the trees on the lot next door. One of them
must be at least a hundred years old. I think they are going to
build a parking lot there.
    —The Reverend Toby Van Buren, minister of the
        Unitarian Church, Baton Rouge, La.

There was a large one
lying on its side—
The years must have slid
                down its back
in ages of silence
and the wind whipped myriads
of throbbing pulse to a lingering branch.

But I am not talking about trees—
with leaves that whisper
meditations to companioned
blackberries and wild daisies.
Nor of the shadowed paths
mostly overgrown with shaggy grass.

Nor am I speaking of the view
from the window—
the forest mimicking distance
and the mystery of unseen boundaries.

I am speaking of the *death* of trees,
which, like all things that die,
tell us of endings—
not necessarily right or wrong,
but quite, quite final.

And even more poignant:
aesthetics dying in the shadowed evening
of a day lost in the artifacts
of paved blocks and measured space.

I am speaking
of the *ghosts* of trees
lending height and breadth
in some immeasurable distance
of the mind and heart.

Nuclear Peril

The light went out
like a thrust of iron
or bone sinking in sand

The hours melt in body
This time I count them
and watch the rain drop
its pellets, heavy as the leafless
limbs swaying downward—
orphaned waifs

> Landscape stretches
> for miles into a gray
> sky   One figure
> silhouettes the dream

Holocaust is no longer real
no longer imagined
no longer one moment
of dread   Consciousness
hangs on the sharp edge
of night   I wait
for a lingering note—
the song, the music
layered somewhere in a burial
of hills

Lost in the solitude
of waiting, I dream
of color, of azaleas
of perfumed gardenias—
Louisiana now a palmetto
uprooted in a dream
of song

Who ravishes
this world, the future an
absence of time? A
spiraling ball takes dominion
writing its brilliant epitaph
in a chain of fire—

I reach for you—
your touch only a memory
a space, a center of space
an absence of space
a song, a dance, a canvas
remembered . . .

Environmental Poem

Remembering the Exxon oil spill in Alaska,
the hundreds of oil wells blown up in Kuwait
during the war with Iraq, and human rape of the earth
and ecological holocaust anywhere

Once more I see songs
in the night air—
piercing, strong, terrible
in their beauty—
fighting against the tyranny,
the dissolution of
   trees
   birds
   houses
   earth
   people

They tell us, these songs,
of a perverse human
spirit transforming the earth
   like dough
   like autumn's grass
   or winter's snow in a season's
   inevitable cycle of movement
   and time

I see your darkness
as change, your sudden
laughter, your convoluted
despair—symbols of the world
at war with itself, turning
into itself, turning upon
itself,
playing checkers with the earth
as if it is some enormous cosmic
game to be resolved and begun
once more,

except that a violated earth
does not cough up again its core.
The ocean wearing a coat of alien
oil, even in its massiveness,
gives up the dead . . .

This spillage of air
and sea and earth-borne
green reaches out to me,
raw bone touching bone,
hands, body, brow,
cheeks, flesh,
already partners in this
grave,

even as I watch the approaching
spreading of light
over a void,
an absence, a space,
a whirling cycle without
    being
    substance
    memory
    weight
    color
    sound
    joy
    life
    death
    existence
    summer
    autumn

or song in a winter's night.

Port Townsend Poems

In memory of Bill Stafford

I. PUGET SOUND. EARLY MORNING

They tell me that the sun
rises from the north
than from the east—
Alaska-borne.

Bright over the sea
it sucks the waves
swelling to shore. No
human voice, no bathers
break the horizon.

Only the gulls, a boat
in the distance, and waist-
high weeds just within reach.

The sky, gray as the waves, flows
into the northern sunrise
that forms a halo
absorbing lowlands and sea,
mountains, and hills.

Clear and without sound
the lighthouse silhouettes
The Point—its vigilant
eye resting now,
waiting, but always

there . . .

II. OUTSIDE MY WINDOW, UNSEEING

Hearing sound I
cannot fathom,
I have visions of fluttering
wings, wet
against wind.

It is the voice of loneliness—
unended, trembling
and dark.

I hear its sad, mindless
music—
waiting . . .

III. COMING HOME

"Good-byes" merge now
like the northern lights.
Was it only yesterday that I
listened to the crows
atop the "Kitchen Shelter"
declaring their presence
to the morning mist
while gulls lined
the curving beach?

I am ready now for home,
for Louisiana lowlands
cropped by pine trees singing
in the wind,
for a house that hums
between rafters and beams,
for caladiums spreading their broad
leaves to a dying sun.

In this northwest town
I will not be missed. But
that's OK. I have felt
the presence of Puget Sound outlining
high bluffs,

> have followed a diagonal sky
> screaming to the sea—curving
> beyond sound and rim,

> have climbed a rugged bank in rain
> and wind—ghosts fading in shade
> and light,

> have listened to poems
> in Bill's workshop—new
> voices, familiar, sculptured
> and fine—

Louisiana, my point of reference,
its moisture, its azaleas, filling the
earth with sweetness and warmth.

MISSISSIPPI RIVER POEMS

The Mississippi rolls
because there are skeletons
rocking in cypress knee chairs
under the silt.
    —Malaika Favorite

I.

The river that divides
but also connects, reaching
from shoreline to bank—
it connects this city to isolation
and rain, rolls silently,
making a path for flotsam and barge,
and light shading light.

"Come quick! The *Delta Queen*
is passing!"

In the night its beams glow
like teeth, each poised
for the bite, like coins,
like Mardi Gras at the height
of the parade—the many-colored
beads thrown to the sky,
to the ground, to hands
clutching for the magic
of connection—human spillage
believing in the promise of
joy.

The Mississippi rolls. The *Delta
Queen,* maiden riverboat
with revelry the norm, passes
in twilight. Laughter spills over
dark water,

the coastline "rocking in cypress
knee chairs under the silt,"
singing their songs of death,
waiting like saints,
waiting like gods,
promising no promises.

The river's chant ringing
forth.

II.

Once I stood on the banks of the river.
The water was green, gray,
the color of grass, the heaviness
of dawn, the ending of twilight,

blackness that soothed
the thickening air, that darkened
the sky, that covered a marsh
no child would explore.

Mornings I surveyed the sparkle,
the surface—beads of ebony
that moved like water snakes,
or sauntered, rasping
in one long breath,
no beginning or end,

a perennial inhaling of light,
or exhaling the dark bowels
of her depths.

A sorceress, purveyor
of seeming, an allusion,
her beauty calls us.

She is grasping, an insatiable
hunger to taste our sweetness
of life.

Her logo is DEATH. Regard
her with caution. She is greedy,
loving, cool,
final.

III.

The Mississippi flows,
touching north side of this campus—
this river—majestic, malignant,
severe in its prescriptive
definition of space.

The grounds of the school
continue to swell. New
growth changes topography
with buildings top-heavy
and wide, devouring air.

But on this side the Mississippi
shields the grounds. No intruders here
except creatures on wings,
bellies, or multiple grasping legs,
or poets looking for a poem.

Wind, rain, gray light
filter through trees at dawn
while shadows at dusk
cradle the songs of birds
and the crickets filling the air
with mating cries:

all respond to the murmur of waves
that turn to the bend of the river
flowing westward and north—
all lost among shadows
of oaks, pines, sycamores lining
the banks that form an impasse
with brambles and brush.

THE RIVER divides,
connects, reflects the sky
absorbing vanishing
light.

III

Songs to the Dialysis Machine

For Ulysses Simpson Lane

DEDICATION

Being woman, I
write this poem
with the voice of woman.
But it is for you, Pete,
man with the proud hate
and circling eyes.
Curse the posture of the chair!
Spit on it! The bastard
mummy hours! Yet
remember: the cold still
blood and the paralytic
limbs would now be legend
were it not for the
machine.

I. INTRO

Nobody knows
what a dialysis machine is,
really,
or cares.
They think
the artificial kidney
is something sewn up
inside you
and works like a clock
or a programmed
computer.

II. THE DIALYSIS MACHINE CALLED THE ARTIFICIAL KIDNEY

Where life is a luxury
and death a dark dream.

It sucks the life-flowing
blood
and sends it back
as a promised gift.
Red, flowing through clear
plastic tubes
like God's river—

this miracle of man's mind.

III. LEG CANNULAS* FOR THE DIALYSIS MACHINE

A rubber stamp day. The sun
as usual a golden spider
creeping to the top of the sky.

Dropping a bottle of cologne
on my foot—
of small import as a rule—
now becomes a Grendel.
My leg gorges herself with bruised
blood and laughs
herself to spikes and needles.

Cannulas clot.

---

*Two plastic tubes inserted under the skin in the arm or leg, one
being attached to the main artery leading to the heart, the other
to the vein leading away from the heart. These are connected to
the arterial and venous tubes of the dialysis machine, which thus
cleanses the blood, doing the work of the kidneys.

I race against time
to deft fingers for irrigating
veins. Bleeding is a luxury
I pray for.

IV. THE HUM OF THE DIALYSIS MACHINE

This humming does not have
the hum of birds
nor is it like the wildly
soft wind.
It does not cup the evening shade
in rock-swollen fields.

Artless, unbroken, without sex
or mind,
it measures life by inches
and is sweet.

If this humming stops
my life ebbs like the tide,
without grace or beauty
though I cling in puzzled anger
to this iron sheath
of day.

V. MOOD

And since each day is a long shadow
stretching the evening,
I let the river of my mind
flow freely.

Each act of will
(courting death)
rides the four winds converging
in a massive

amber whirlpool of yellow light.
Each day lies suspended
beneath unhinged
loops of rope.

Unsmiling time
unbeating hearts
ungrasping hands
slide round the yellow wind
and bolts slip out of place
beneath the sun.

VI. BACK AGAIN

I fight for life
and put my whole weight
against the door of death.
Stubbornly I cling
to this semi-brightness
this façade of existence.

The vagueness of "unsmiling time"
becomes a clock-hour day
measured in minutes and seconds.
I see in reverse
all the passing years.

"Live one day at a time,"
they tell me. "Let the future
take care of itself."

Can one corner time
and seal it in a jar
like a bottled insect?

The day is not suspended now,
but is a block of ice
beneath my feet.
Each frozen hour
waits for spring
and the melting season.

Love Poems: Epitaph for the Blues

I. AWAKENING

It is time for a poem.
I know the time
when sleepless nights and beating
of the heart
ring tones of troubled mind—
vague, like an offshore hollow voice,
deep, deep as the light in your eyes,
Love.

It is time for a poem—
diamond-cased and unapproachable things,
sinewed-strung.

(Dare I sing this song?)

Once I was so sure of what was
right and what was wrong,
could have laid down golden rules
that say: "This is the line
one must not cross."
How beautiful and simple.
How uncomplex.

Darkness gathers brightly
and my demon starlets dance
like tinseled ghosts on a saint's night.

Don't speak to me of what is wrong
or right—
your law voices and your Janus faces—
in my heart I know:
right is what hurts others least.

My human frailness plunged
in blossoms of spring
drowns in the ocean's
sweet and pungent depths.

This poem is for you, love.

II. WHAT DOES ONE SAY TO THE MAD?

> What does one say to the mad? They hang
> From their trees like swollen fruit, unwilling
> To fall . . .
> —Charles Wright

What does one say to the mad?
To the mad hate, the mad pain,
the mad, mad love?

Listening shadows glance off the wall,
hiding past my mad new day—
what does one say to this mad new love,
Love?
Tell me.

III. DESPAIR

> The day of my soul is
> the nature of that
> place. It is a landscape. Seen
> from the top of a hill.
> —LeRoi Jones

Love,
the top of the hill is
the lower waiting place
of my days and nights. The
day sings darkly
like crickets in
the swollen grass.

It is hopeless, yes.
And I curse my mind's lament—
so silly and so foul.

The iron gate hangs slantingly,
neither letting in nor letting out.

Once I hid in an alcove
and let the night air
filter past my screaming eyes
shut against the wind.

The days are warmer now.
And I see your face
glowing like the sun.

The mirror hurls back
the falling day pulling
down the sky.
I sit and listen
to the stillness of my lips,
then murmur wordlessly.

The night canvasses
the howling of my bursting
flesh,
and nothing stops this idiotic reverie,
this song's lament.

IV. BEYOND WORDS

Flesh
has a way
of reaching out
past pawn, tricks,
sophistication—

an articulation
beyond compare.

All my words now seem
but the babblings
of an idiot
before the eloquence
of flesh
that speaks a poem
in the darkness
glancing off the soft light
creeping past our limbs
and soaking up
the night.

V. FOR A FUTURE'S TREASURY

> . . . we feel enough left there
> In our commotion to stir the spirit
> As well as the flesh.
> —Carl Bode

The spirit and the mind, yes—a prelude,
an overture. Our gliding on the lawn,
folding in tufts of grass.

Music tumbling in drifts
of wind
and spilled sky dropping threads of
water in a summer's light.

Your smile was etched against the sun
with rays ricocheting across my fluttering pulse:
manna for the spirit—
our weaving webs of memory
stored for a future's treasury . . .

And *love* on an afternoon
balanced firmly on the days
of heart.

VI. "WRITE ME A POEM."

And yet there were times
when sun turned to willows,
light burned to ashes,
and I became a melting candle.

One word, one look, one smile—
and *day*
opened up—a sea of
blinding light.

Tumbling in orbit,
I did not *fall* in love:
I *flowed* into it
gently, firmly pulled,
my own volition
notwithstanding.

VII. FOR YOU

A brisk walk
on a half-cold
September day

and suddenly
a breeze capering
against the back
of my hand.

I loved you like
a sudden wind.
Bright-eyed fear

and wonder
tossed in the dark—
warm, edged with
sleeplessness
and disbelief.

"We cannot be all
of everything to one another,"
you said. Dear,
I know.
Neither can the rain
fill rivers
or sun stir sleepers
from the pit.

We cannot be all
of everything,
but let the
fragments be jewels
of light
and embers glowing
in the dark,
and love a catalyst
against an endless, aching
night.

VIII. VIGNETTES

(Suddenly)
there you were,
your voice
reaching out to me
over layers of
loneliness
and years of space.

(Reality)
has a hard
cruel surface. At home
I face his cynic voice,
his sardonic, crisp
glittering words of hate.
And I run like hell
to escape his rage of
fear
his hard round cage of
ice.

❧

("I love loving you,"
you said.)
A liaison of
feeling stretched
across the highways
of our
minds.

❧

(Mood)
Shifting vessels
bending with
each day's demise,
merging into the
design of things
like forms on canvas.

❧

(My fear)
Nothing
lasts forever . . .

not love
nor hate
nor need, desire
fire
ice

❧

(What drew me to you?)
An impishness?
A devilish sparkle
of the eye?

There is a glow about you
a vitality
a boyishness
an unbelievable kindness
a humane empathy
a glorious enclosing spirit of
love.

❧

(We are)
lost
in the space of Time—
singing like spring robins.
Dying
        Dying
                Dying.
But
holding to the sun's
edge,

dangling on the fringe
of night.

IX. WAITING OUT THE DAYS

We don't want the days
to become staple
like jelly or bread.

Let our knowing one another
be excitement
passion
palpitation of the pulse
and all those things
that make our loving
a streak of lightning
an extraordinary thing.

Even agony
is better than boredom
and uncertainty
a tower over dull predictability,

wouldn't you say?

X. COMMUNICATION

Let us
      not
     lose
    the voice
   that holds us
  together.

No magical string
holds the heart.
Like any vital organ
it has logical
connections—vessels
leading in and leading
out.

Nothing from nothing
leaves nothing
and a vacuum is only itself . . .

The voice
is our heart's vessel.

Love.

XI. COFFEE HOUR

carried me miles and miles offshore.

Once I tried floating back
like a dead fish.
I even tried swimming.
The best thing to do
is to lay the belly flat
and drink the waves.

(We merge with land and sea and sky,
disappear in air.)

You were there, your flesh
wrapped in shirt and tie and tweed.
Coffee singed my lips,
and I sighed contentedly.

XII. SHADOWS

Danger follows, lurking in walls.
It seeps in stairways, lines
doorways and halls. Once
I thought I saw his form
trailing like a malignant seeker
after what is lost,
forever gone.

What does he hope to gain?
Does he think to resurrect ghosts
of the past? To chain a spirit?
What gravity does he think
will pull us down together to the suction earth?

Does he believe we will rise like angels
and sweep away the shit years?
Perhaps he thinks they never happened?

    Fool!
    Don't you know that nothing
    remains the same?
    That the line between us
    grows interminably long,
    and that any direction
    is better than none at all?

XIII. GRIEFS OF JOY

No, nothing remains the same.
And my spirit reaches out to you,
My Love,
without apologies
without embarrassment
with only the thought that this is
right for us
that moving towards you is like
touching leaves in autumn
or reading Yeats and Cummings
together on a special night—

my chin grazing your neck
as you glide through
my father moved though dooms of love
while "our sames of am and haves of give"

give measures of light drifting
through our "griefs of joy,"
our minds and spirits
interlocked like death.

The splendor of the moment
moves quietly, softly, calmly
without fuss or bother
to some point of unforgetfulness
and love.

XIV. LOVING

Looped in each other's arms
without thought of endings,
we are sure only
of the reality of the moment.
Morals are a private affair,
 and "hell," said Faustus,
"is but a fable."

To avoid banality, we lock
the silence in
with only low tones of the record player
moaning irreverent music—sounds
sucked into the low light
seeping through the half-drawn shades.

Let's not rush toward
our own destruction.

This moment's dying cauterizes death
and breathes life into the sinews
strung together.

XV. A BACKWARD LOOK

> We in love skate
> over the knuckles of others.
> —Joyce Carol Oates

Without meaning to, of course,
but it is inevitable.
Light descends
and blindingly blanks the path.
We are diffused into all of it.
We try evaluating this
and weighing that—
are sure we are being quite
intelligent about it all.
But when the passage clears a little
we see trickles of blood
staining the back trail.
"The knuckles were in the way,"
we say.
No, not really. We
just refused to see them.

XVI. APPREHENSION

I am cold sometimes
and tremble.
I am afraid—not of the dark
or even of the half-demolished shade
but only of the possibility
of the terrible, terrible
void
that in the wake
you will be gone
that your structured years
descending
will engulf you.

I live now only for each day
overwhelmed by every moment.
The future is a dim harbor
that I don't even try to fathom.

XVII. FINIS

Should this final poem
be sad?
But it is not
and what I feel for you
is whole, and
real
a moving in and out of the beauty of you,
a private joy of knowing you and
growing
into you.

It is time to stop the lines.
But love lives on.

XVIII. POSTSCRIPT

And there is no finality.

My home was in your smile
and in the comfort
of your voice—
each day a pendant
between love and pain.

I, selfish
in my enclosing,
grasp the ever-loosening
threads . . .

This final word—the hour
of knowing that only with
uninhibited air can we survive.
The ashes now lie
on the ground.

You have taught me
the meaning of final
unremitting pain.

XIX. SUNRISE

I don't try now to push
the days into corners.
The leaves drift aimlessly,
your voice lost and cold.
I see your eyes in patches
of blue spotted through the trees
or wet paint bright on canvas.
Your smile hangs loosely
in my mind's recess.

An oriole flits to the ground. His
restless energy saddens me
for he has what I lack:
the will to rip paths in air
and slice his mind with doing.

But I lie here quietly,
a soft mass yielding
to the light molding your form,
and slip into shadows
until sunrise returns to our
once spoken words of heart.

XX. AN AFTERTHOUGHT

I thought I had run
out of words about you
but warm blood and
cold air have no
finality beyond themselves.
And in the rush of work hours,
in the blare of television that
cuts through stillness,
in liquid air
you hover like remnants
of years past
or light laced by a moving cloud
across my sky.

If I reach deep enough
I'll grasp more distance
than I care to think about
and if I cry far enough
I'll float into the future's
weightlessness
and dissolve
without a whimper.

XXI. HEALING

> And when the winds come
> I shall cry a little for the pain in them
> —Peter Dechert

But I shall sit without mourning
to watch the sky
return to form.

I think, I really think, I shall
love you always.
But if forgetfulness sets in,

let it be by permission
of deep shadows
in the everglades low-lying
in that realm of memory
not quite touching "gone."

And let the winds come cleanly,
not like falling leaves,
but like the drift of wild geese
sweeping on with grace.

And let our having loved
be dusk and late harvest songs
though

       I shall cry a little
       for the pain.